rock flight

rock flight

Hasib Hourani

A New Directions Paperbook Original

Published by arrangement with Giramondo Publishing Company, Penrith, NSW, Australia

Design by Eileen Bellamy
Manufactured in the United States of America
First published as a New Directions Paperbook (NDP1628) in 2025

Library of Congress Cataloging-in-Publication Data
Names: Hourani, Hasib, 1996– author.
Title: Rock flight / Hasib Hourani.
Description: New York, NY : New Directions Publishing Corporation, 2024. | "A New Directions paperbook original".
Identifiers: LCCN 2024045631 | ISBN 9780811238854 (paperback) | ISBN 9780811238861 (ebook)
Subjects: LCGFT: Poetry.
Classification: LCC PR9619.4.H68 R63 2024 | DDC 821/.92—dc23/eng/20241114
LC record available at https://lccn.loc.gov/2024045631

10 9 8 7 6 5 4 3 2 1

New Directions Books are published for James Laughlin
by New Directions Publishing Corporation
80 Eighth Avenue, New York 10011

ndbooks.com

the Palestinians are dumped in a space-craft heading for the moon
They sing their own requiem in the launched rocket
piloted by the angels of EVIL in outer Space they get lost
stone has no memory   STOP   the sun neither   STOP
                                    —Etel Adnan, *The Arab Apocalypse*

rock flight

–ī: the arabic suffixation that turns a word into an ethnonym

ethnonym: the name applied to a given ethnic or cultural group

houran: syria's south to jordan's north directly east of palestine.
within houran: a field of 118 basaltic volcanoes and
within that field: mount
houran
1800M

one

five months old and in flight. five months old by a window that doesn't open because it's been engineered not to. high altitude makes my throat blister and then crunch, swallow, crunch. born flying and landing and flying again. dizzy and trying to find the nearest chemist in between a flight and a train ride. a chemist to soothe the bile pushing against my throat. my throat that is boarded shut and popping.

in this text unless the context otherwise requires:

"it" means the reason i am elsewhere

"thing" means the reason i am elsewhere

"israel" means the reason i am elsewhere

"something" means the reason i am elsewhere

"entity" means the reason i am elsewhere

"██████████████████████████████" means the reason i am elsewhere

"the suffocating state" means the reason i am elsewhere

1. cutting off its air supply is not murder because
    a. you're almost dead
    b. the thing shouldn't exist

strangle	strangle	strangle		strangle
strangle	strangle	strangle		no
that's	not the	right	word	
	maybe	the	word	i'm
	thinking of	is	suffocate	no
maybe	that's not	right		either

i just want to cut off its circulation until it says
give me back my oxygen
and i will say *no*

2. nothing ever really stops existing
    a. even if you kill it
        i. this is a good thing because we do not want to die
        ii. this is a bad thing because burning a flag is not enough
    b. so why bother killing it?

those spiky little balls in mountain grass
whose name i do not know
and i will never know
because i will never look it up
because that is not my secret and i am not nosy

stuck to the cuff of my jeans. following me all the way to the
harbor. stuck to the sleeve of my pink jacket. pulling something
up almost all the way.

3. a pillar holds something up
   a. until it falls
   b. is five of them overdoing it?
      i. no
   c. but what makes a pillar a pillar?

a rock

rubble makes a thing holy because
you go to a place and say
this was worth fighting over
and you are not half wrong

two rocks side by side

eventually the rubble stops counting for all that much
because green grows thick through and over
and you can start lying
we're rebuilding

a handful of rocks laid flat

JANNAH meaning heaven
heaven is full of flowers
the universe is a garden

a pile of rocks

JNAYNAH meaning garden
named as such because you're pretty
close to heaven but not quite there yet

a mound of rocks

JENIN as in the city
it's full of farmland and
if you are from there
your world is a garden

one more rock
right on the top

    if it stays put: a mountain
if it topples over: a dismantling

    4. what warrants a war?
      a. beauty (my dad said this)

my grandparents flee the beauty. it's 1948. they are on foot until
they reach the refugee camp in aleppo and then they meet. they
have five children and they're all born stateless. myself and most
of my cousins are born stateless too refugees by inheritance. we
now have five nationalities between us passports that allow us
to move and move and move again some more freely than
others. none of us have palestinian citizenship. my grandfather
fled the living in 2015 my grandmother in 2021 they were my
last bloodline that belonged to palestine on paper.

i'm in my twenties with my parents and siblings we are trying
to go home just for ten days. we are in a black minivan and i
spend three hours in the back seat saying: *i don't get it.* and
when i get to jenin i say: *i still don't get it.* i reach the camp and i
say: *you're not doing a very good job at explaining it to me.* and
then my sister shows me a video she took somewhere along the
drive and it's several minutes long and, because the car was
moving so fast, it's just a horizontal blur of green and i say:
where was i when this was happening? but not out loud.

5. nothing ever really stops existing
  a. this means that nothing ever really stops happening
    i. this means that even when you are not in the right
      place at the right time, you'll still be there
      ı. you are always there

those spiky little balls in mountain grass
splintered into your finger tips
forever pricking every thing you touch

man of stone man of mud man of
slip
remember my body when it leaves
if you are afraid that the last rock will ruin everything it
already has

EMPTY:
meaning something is not occupied. this is from an internet
dictionary but who trusts dictionaries or the internet? and the
more time i spend with words the more i realize that they do
not mean anything at all. a rock is not a rock until it's thrown.

HOW TO MAKE A ROCK
please find a piece of paper

ONE
scrunch it up

TWO
throw it

i can't remember jericho all that well
but i remember the windows
in houses
in rocks
in mountains
i remember the rocks
i remember the rock flour
the sand

and now i am at my dining table
in brunswick west
short of breath
making lists

in 2005 palestinian civil-society organizations call for boycott
divestment and sanctions to choke israel back. there are three
demands:

end the occupation and colonization of all arab lands
and dismantle the apartheid wall

recognize the fundamental rights of the arab-palestinian citizens
to full equality
1/5 of israel's citizens are palestinians who remained
inside the armistice lines after 1948
they are subjected to systemic racial
discrimination enshrined in over 50 laws

enforce the right of return to all palestinian refugees[1]

1   Palestinian Civil Society, "Palestinian Civil Society Call for BDS," *BDS Movement*
(July 9, 2005). Accessed November 2021: https://bdsmovement.net/call.

it's good
it works
among other things
like fire

it worked in the sixties
it worked when they did it in south africa in the sixties

my eyes are red hot and wet my whole life. sometimes i kick
the pavement like it owes me something and sometimes i
dribble onto the low pile carpet of my bedroom. most of the
time i am bilal: on my back, bloated sun, boulder on bare chest.
they say *stop your calls to action* and i say *no*.

   6. what's the word i'm looking for?
     a. asphyxiate
     b. choke
     c. suppress
     d. snuff

HOW TO HOLD YOUR BREATH

ONE
take your right hand
use your index finger and your thumb
to pinch your nostrils shut

TWO
take your left hand
place the palm over your mouth
use lots of force to make sure
no air can come in or out

THREE
make your lungs stop moving

NOTE
if you are my mother don't worry about steps ONE through
THREE you know how to hold your breath without doing
anything at all

one more

we cannot live like this but it can
i want it to not be able to live like this either
i want it to say *give me back my oxygen*
i want it to say *something needs to change*
i want it to do the changing

trrrraaaaapppppppppeeeeedddddd
make the noise
           sound
like a creak haunting i
want it to feel trapped

a rock painted pretty, light blue,
it holds open the door to the living room

hp

   provides
   maintains
   controls
      ١* the identification system in israel[2]
      ٢* the control mechanism at checkpoints[3]
      ٣* administration for their navy's IT infrastructure[4]
      ٤* digital storage systems for their illegal settlements[5]

2   Who Profits, *Technologies of Control: The Case of Hewlett Packard,* "Stratified
    Identities: the New ID Cards System" (Tel Aviv: Who Profits, 2011), 16–17.

3   Who Profits, *Technologies of Control,* "OK Computer: The Basel Biometric
    Checkpoint System," 9–11.

4   Who Profits, *Technologies of Control,* "Smart Occupation: HP's Contracts with
    the Israeli Army," 20–22.

5   Who Profits, *Technologies of Control,* "No Boundaries: HP's Activities in the Israeli
    Settlements," 25.

١* it takes seven years. out of 27 companies, hp's offer was the
only one to comply with the ministry of interior's public tender
٢* it reads facial dimensions and hand geometry

٣* this infrastructure was a pilot program for implementing the
same system into the entire army
٤* and the mayor said that without this system, the settlement
could never have advanced into a city

do you   trust technology   ?

            see why i don't

i am at the center of something and yes, i can break through
the plastic barrier of the thing i'm in but then i will just be
trapped again, this time in something bigger, and this process
will go on and on like a perfectly looped video: i am in a fleshy
circle; i shed the fleshy circle; i notice a papery film closing in
on me; i am being shellpacked again.

this is how i feel about politics and echo chambers

blocked up with black dirt trying to come up for air

little onion hearts
pervasive
and they keep for forever
and then you add fire
a second life covered in soot
and they are like molasses: sweet
and they are like butter: slipping in and out of things

when i am in palestine i wake up every day to the smell of sugar
from the bakeries downstairs and i feel sick like i am going to vomit

i live in a different colony to the one suffocating us. i fly one hour
and take the train for two. i am on a writing residency to work
on this book that you are reading. it rains most days but that is
OK. there is a ghost in my bedroom but that is OK too. i don't
realize it's a ghost until afterwards. it opens my closet in the
middle of the night but closes it again before sunrise. it spends
the first night sleeping on my chest so that i cannot move or sit up.

i am still at the residency but it's two days later. i read a book on
knowledge and the author has been in this house too and he has
seen this ghost too. he says: *i won a fellowship to do a writing
retreat for a week at* ███████ he says: *there are settler ghosts here
where i am writing and they are angry as hell* he says *the other
authors are experiencing things* he says: *one of them spent two nights
with something sitting on her chest so that she couldn't move.*

if i want to wake up and drive from beirut where my mum is
from to the galilee where my dad is from i would have to drive
seven hours. i would need two passports. they are 100KM apart
but still i would have to drive seven hours with a passport in each
hand and two hands on the wheel. from lebanon across to syria
syria down into jordan jordan back over to palestine. our fight
does not hit a frail and hand-drawn border and halt. it passes
through the levant and turns 100KM into 400 instead.

i am home from the residency on sunday night and on monday
morning i am the first person in the office. all the desks have
new monitors on them and we have new laptops too.

the monitors
and laptops
and servers
they are hp

a strip of tape over
a cardboard box of foam
protecting a plastic sleeve
then a laptop

my ears and armpits are hot
i am setting up a fingerprint passcode
                              and now hp has my finger
            and the army that chokes us has my finger
            and the police that chokes us has my finger
                              and my finger
                        is on a list somewhere
so i go to the settings and then
DELETE

HOW TO MAKE A BOX
please find a piece of paper

ONE

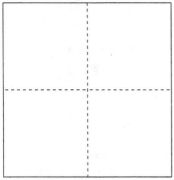

fold the paper in half one way
then fold it in half the other way

TWO

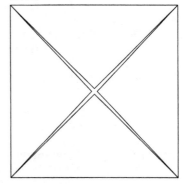

use the grooves from step one and
fold the corners into the center

THREE

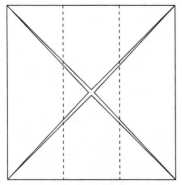

fold the new smaller square
into thirds one way

FOUR

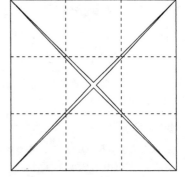

now fold it into thirds the
other way

FIVE

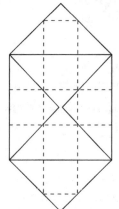

SIX

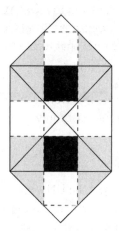

unfold the top and bottom flaps

fold the shaded sections into
the colored-in sections

SEVEN

pinch the edges of your box to make
sure everything stays in place
close the lid and keep it that way

i want you to recall all the pictures
of   pelicans   after   an   oil   spill
the ones that went viral for a week
then stopped circulating

because traveling when you're coated in thick diesel slip
cannot last forever. we get tired. we all have to land eventually.

a rock isn't a rock   until it is thrown

in 1948 the UN general assembly passes a resolution they say
any palestinian refugees who want to return to their homes
should be permitted to do so. they also mention money they
say that compensation must be paid for the property of those
choosing not to return and for the loss of or damage to proper-
ty. my great grandmother zahra owns one hundred dunams of
land in jish in palestine and on it: groves of olive trees. her sons
flee but she stays with the beauty and waits for her sons to
come back.

   7. stop moving around so much
       a. are you trying to go home?
           i. yes
               ١. so … you're finding somewhere new?
               ٢. so … you're returning?
           ii. no
               ١. good

israel is rejecting 7.2 million palestinians the right of return. i am part of the 7.2 million and together we are two thirds of all palestinians in the world. zahra flees the living in 1971 and the beauty is still in her name but her sons can't go back and can't claim it. my dad meets a lawyer one summer and asks for his help but it goes nowhere.

an airport scale
of one to six
and getting marked six every time
so your bag is checked your person
is checked your
background is checked[6]
they like to make you feel
humiliated
    it's deterrence and
    it works

at karameh bridge we are held
till nearly sunset and
my dad is sick
my skin hurts
the only other family given as hard a time as us
are two parents and their teenage daughter
they are black south african
my brother never wanted to come

---

6   Omar Barghouti, *Boycott, Divestment, Sanctions: The Global Struggle for Palestinian Rights*, "Reflecting on the Cultural Boycott" (Chicago: Haymarket Books, 2011), 132–133.

now i am on the M1
with my sister
her name is jeanine like the place and she has green eyes
and i am still trying to find the word:

        STRANGLE; CHOKE; THROTTLE; PRESSURE;
        SUPPRESS; STRAIN; CONSTRAIN; BURDEN;
        SQUEEZE; PRESS; PUSH; FORCE; URGE

hold your breath, where's that box you made? put this book inside and close the lid. when you need to come up for air, open the box and keep reading.

one more rock

8. cutting off its air supply is not murder
    a. when the thing is a murderer
    b. when you are being choked

i'm with campfire
    and smoke
    with out phone reception
pewter grey roaming settling roaming
settling
my eyes sting my chest is thick
a boyfriend says
████████████
and ███████████
and then ██████████
and then █████████████████████████
i'm with campfire
    and smoke
    with out phone reception
    and a boyfriend
    not mine thank god

```
i    am   in   a  box   now
and the box is a yellow dumpster
on    jamal abdel nasser  street
i    am    a    cattle   egret
in    a    yellow    dumpster
on    jamal abdel nasser  street
i    am    a    water    bird
and  jenin  is  forty  kilometers
from                      water
in    either          direction
```

i am in front of a mirror. and by that i mean i am the cattle egret in the yellow dumpster and i am also a passenger in a black minivan looking at the cattle egret in the yellow dumpster. so as a promise not to forget and because i am young and enjoy metaphors, i ink the cattle egret on my right leg forever and say *when i move you move* and again i make a promise. i will lead the bird back to water. but instead i spend one year deciding not to go anywhere and the next two governmentally prohibited from going anywhere.

9. what's a box?
    a. a cage for things that aren't living
        i. a closet
        ii. a silo
        iii. the skin of an onion
        iv. a coffin
    b. four walls a floor and a ceiling
    c. something that stops you from moving
        i. a hall of mirrors
        ii. a slippery floor
        iii. breathlessness

sometimes i am in front of the bathroom mirror and someone is
saying: *you look like a falcon*

sometimes i am breathless and someone is saying: *you look like
a falcon with your eyes and your beak*

in another life i am pecking through overgrown green
and in this life i cannot breathe because i'm blocked up with
black dirt
    in this life i cannot breathe because sometimes
    i pick through black dirt but it is actually wet cement
    and it sticks
    and it dries
    and not only am i blocked up, i am weighed down

karim flies three hours to stay with his auntie and cousins for
two weeks and in his suitcase: two 10KG dumbbells and enough
underwear for the trip. my teen theory is that he's going through
something right now and because of that he's on edge and
because of that he needs to always be ready. twenty kilograms
to protect him, twenty kilograms to weigh him down.

twenty kilograms on a trachea and a veiny hand to bind them

macaws eat seeds that are toxic. and afterwards they gather on
mounds of clay like it's rite. and they sit. and they lick. and the
clay adsorbs what would have otherwise killed them. and the
clay sits in their belly like its rite.

clay to protect the new world birds. clay to weigh them down.

    10. reasons to feed clay to pigeons:
        a. it's the great depression and clay slows them down
           i. now they're easier to catch and there's food on the table

b. it's world war ii and clay weighs them down
   i. now they can't bother the pilots
c. your bullets are made of clay
   i. go on, shoot

HOW TO MAKE ANOTHER BOX

ONE
take your right hand
use your index finger and your thumb
to pinch your nostrils shut

TWO
take your left hand
place the palm of it over your mouth
use lots of force to make sure
that no air can come in or out

THREE
make your lungs stop moving

11. what's a box?
    a. something that stops you from moving
        i. oil-slick in your wings
        ii. fractured bones
        iii. clay in your belly
        iv. a box with no air-holes

NESTING:
  i make it
          so that that every place i live is my home so
  i put my bed on the wall closest to the window, always
  furthest from the door,   always
  i keep my window open,   always
except the one in this new place has been painted shut
and there is nothing sharp enough to chip away
at the vinyl that lacquers me vacuum-packed

heaviest in the morning man
of stone man of slip
man unable to lift
the limbs that spent the night settling
speak
remember my body when it leaves

everything is dough if you're strong enough
take a boulder and shape it
after fire it's whatever you made it

everything is dough if you're strong enough
eat the window open

a man on the street is trying to sell me something anything he
can think of a rock pure gold a postage stamp a feather he says
twenty shekel twenty shekel just twenty shekel and i wake up
with red dots on my arms and legs. loose bed sheets. i think i
have bed bugs. home intruders. i think of jericho and i think of
it again and i think of it again: a video on loop and i can't get
back to sleep.

those spiky little balls in mountain grass
splintered into your finger tips
now your wingspan ends sharp

   sometimes i want to wake up early and be the bird that wins
sometimes i want to be the worm that says: *just five more minutes*

every autumn and every spring half a billion birds pass over
palestinian air. the air is contested, they can't get home. the
suffocating state has a solution: a 1991 military initiative titled
migrating birds know no boundaries. the campaign is twee it
uses the phrase *take care we share the air*. so the suffocating state
bans low-altitude flight during peak spring and fall migration.
there are no-go zones they call them *bird-plagued*. collisions
between birds and planes fall by 76 percent and the suffocating
state has saved raptor lives. thank you suffocating state for
saving raptor lives.

12. what do zionists consider contested?
    a. west bank
    b. east jerusalem
    c. gaza
    d. syrian golan heights
but the whole of palestine is colonized
not just the beauty annexed after 1967

sometimes i want to wake up and drive from beirut to the galilee
              i want the region back unfractured
                          like it was before

because we can't get palestine back
                    until i can drive from beirut to the galilee
                    and maybe we'll have a bullet train

a guest lecturer at my CWRI course teaches us to eradicate
animal idioms from our language because they are cruel she
uses *two birds one stone* as an example

i am twenty-two and email a professor from tel aviv university
because i think *there's no harm in trying* and i make my project
sound ambiguous
i say:

        i'm a freelance writer and amateur
        birder... i'm writing about birds
        and migration... as an *audobon*
        subscriber i've come across your
        projects in a number of articles
        and am so fascinated by the
        "migrating birds know no
        boundaries" initiative... i've been
        trying rigorously for weeks to find
        information about the program (its

conception,   implementation   in
schools)... the specific aspects
that interest me are the ones
mentioned in the following article:
and i give him the URL to the article but he doesn't reply maybe
he doesn't even see the email maybe it goes straight to junk and
automatically kills itself off after thirty days maybe he does read
it maybe he skims it scoffs and then DELETE

maybe he doesn't trust technology
                              or emails
from strangers especially when they have links to click

the project i'm working on kills itself off, too
it takes about a year

israeli soldiers wear tee-shirts off-duty
a sharpshooter from the givati brigade
wears one that says *one shot two kills*
and then an image of a pregnant palestinian woman
and a bulls-eye on her belly[7]

---

7   Uri Blau, "Dead Palestinian Babies and Bombed Mosques—IDF Fashion 2009,"
     Haaretz (March 19, 2009). Accessed March 2021: https://www.haaretz.com/
     2009-03-19/ty-article/dead-palestinian-babies-and-bombed-mosques-idf-fashion-
     2009/0000017f-e11a-d568-ad7f-f37b4fd90000.

HOW TO MAKE A THROAT
please find a piece of paper

ONE
scrunch it up

one more rock thrown

i see a photo of a great heron eating a rat head first. it's nine in
the morning a film of mucus doming my fried egg and i feel
sick like i am going to vomit. now it is on my tongue now it is
caught between molars chewing swallowing swallow sinking
into the pit of the gut.

dirty water of the aqueduct
near my house it collects the downpour
                    it walks me down
the citylink
               funneling downward downhill
waterlog the cement throat
vomit into the stream

eat a date
keep the stone
put it in your pocket

in the olden days the arab sailors were the only sailors who did
not contract scurvy while at sea. they were still getting vitamin
c from the dates they packed. i do not fact check this because i
trust my dad.[8]

if you are on your deathbed lying on the sand, plant a date
before your last breath and you will go straight to heaven١*. i
do not fact check this because my teacher scares me.

١* anas ibn mailk reports that rasool allah pbuh said, *even if the
resurrection were established upon one of you while he has in his
hand a sapling, let him plant it.*[9]

---

8   jeanine reads my manuscript in draft form to check the political messaging and
    highlights the word "dad" and comments "pretty sure i told him that story."

9   "Hadith on Trees," *Daily Hadith Online: The Teachings of Prophet Muhammad.*
    Accessed November 2022, https://www.abuaminaelias.com/dailyhadithon-
    line/2012/11/24/plant-tree-ressurection/.

وَأَرْسَلَ عَلَيهِم طَيْرًا أَبَابِيلَ

and	he	delivers	unto	them	birds	in	flocks
	god	issues	to		aves		droves
		orders	onto				masses
		dispatches	upon				clusters

تَرمِيهِم بِحِجَارَةٍ مِّن سِجِّيل

throwing	at	them	stones	of	clay
casting			rocks	from	
launching					
shooting					
flinging					
slinging					

i am walking down the street and there is a rock on the
pavement and look another one. the first city i see when
i see palestine is jericho. we are driving down a flat wide
road in a straight line, boulders and hollows on either side
and i'm thinking *yes i made it* and then *yes i get it now* because it
is about the earth. it has always been about the earth.

the jewish ethnostate was thought up by someone else
the french and the british
1799[10] one hundred years
before zionism two hundred years
before ███████████████████████████████

    13. did you have a rock in your pocket?
        a. yes
            i. did you throw it?
                ١. yes
                    ١. with the intent to seriously harm?
                        a. yes
                            i. twenty years away
                        b. no
                            i. ten years away
                ٢. no
        b. no

it's not enough
it won't do
we can't only choke
back the state that chokes us when
      the state that chokes us
is being breathed alive
   by bigger empires
               empires that created
      the state that chokes us
to keep the empires
         empires

---

10 Abdul-Wahhab Kayyali, *Zionism, Imperialism, and Racism*, "The Historial Roots of
the Imperialist-Zionist Alliance" (London: Croom Helm, 1979), 9–24.

god created the earth and said, *gibril go plant these stones all over it,*
and gibril took them and because we live on a sphere the rocks
spread like butter: evenly, melting. and then gibril tripped on
the taut string border into palestine and his bag of rocks spilled
and now our country is a monument of stones, and a garden of
stones, and a reminder of *do not fall over.* a reminder of *when you
are fleeing, look to your feet.*

eat a date
keep the stone
in your pocket: the weight of the afterlife
                              of ammunition

              a rock isn't a rock

                                        until it is thrown

                              and then it is a weapon

                        and then you are put into a box

what a throat
on that waterbird
to eat a rat whole

HOW TO MAKE A ROCK

ONE
eat a date

HOW TO MAKE A SLING

ONE
rest the pit of the date
gently on your tongue

TWO
open your mouth
the width of a finger

THREE
blow whip-sharp and fast
like storm
like current

one more rock thrown
onto the pile

stay put
a child-sized chair fifteen centimeters high
with the front legs or the back legs
shortened it gives the seat a slope
the seat is twenty centimeters
by twenty centimeters and it is sloped
sit down
stay put on the sloped child-sized chair
stay there for two days
the child-sized chair is fixed to the floor by a long padlock
if the slope is a backwards slope
the back rest cuts into you
if the slope is a forwards slope
it's your thighs instead
nettled by sweat and dirt
stay there for two days and do not fall asleep
there is a hood and loud music
and do not fall asleep

fifty centimeters wide
one meter long you do not know how high
a narrow room it is so so narrow
it is called a closet
sometimes the closet
is called a grave it is the size of a witness stand
and there is a pool
that smells rancid
and the pool is put there on purpose
fifty centimeters wide and hot
and stuffy
but sometimes
it is fitted with cooling systems
and fixed with rubber around the door
and then the closet
is called a refrigerator instead
fifty centimeters wide
one meter long and made of cement
no windows no where for air to come in
unless the closet is a refrigerator and then
the air is fake
sometimes the child-sized chair
is padlocked into the closet of all places so you
stay put for two days and do not fall asleep
in the sloped chair in the closet that is
sometimes called a grave
stay put fifty centimeters
wide one meter long and hold your breath
because it is rancid
and you cannot breathe because it is hot
and stuffy do not fall asleep

TORTURE METHODS EMPLOYED
BY THE STATE OF ISRAEL[11]

sensory deprivation
       placing detainees in strict isolation
       placing detainees in extreme cold
       placing detainees in suffocating heat
       placing foul-smelling hoods over detainees' faces to
       induce feeling of suffocation

psychological pressures
       inducing feelings of exhaustion
       inducing feelings of disorientation
       inducing feelings of dread
       depriving detainees of sleep
       broadcasting loud and jarring music around the clock
       restricting access to the toilet
       forcing detainees to eat in toilet stalls
       forcing detainees to relieve themselves in their clothing

11   Human Rights Watch: Middle East, *Torture and Ill-Treatment: Israel's Interrogation of Palestinians from the Occupied Territories* (Washington: Human Rights Watch, 1994).

beating and physical force
     repeated choking
     beatings and kicks to the
          throat
          groin
          stomach
     slamming detainees' heads against the wall
     violent shaking by the shoulders or the collar to induce
          severe neck pain
          severe back pain
          choking sensation
          whiplash

GSS interrogators beat detainees less often than they did in the past. the GSS now relies more on position abuse and sensory deprivation to wear down detainees. less violent methods leave less compelling physical evidence of abuse, making it more difficult for victims to prove the abuse and prosecute the abusers.

position abuse
  forcing detainees into prolonged standing
      shackling detainees to pipes or rings at
      awkward heights
  forcing detainees into prolonged sitting
      shackling detainees into tiny chairs often angled
      downward or upward
  confining detainees in small enclosed spaces to induce
      circulatory problems
      backaches
      abrasions
      severe cramps
      loss of sensation in the limbs

one more rock thrown
onto the pile to tumble
the mountain

delete all material from a space, hollow out a room. this is a blank slate, this is beginning again. this is a good thing. delete all material from a space, this is a blank slate, this is beginning again. hollow out a room and sound cannot travel through it.

test it out by saying the word KNUCKLE

empty out a box and fill it with only the letters K through O

test it out by saying the word KN   KL

test it out by saying the word LO   K

test it out by saying the word   OL   MN

test it out by saying the word

test it out by saying the word KNO   K

delete all material from a space and the ghost of it remains

    13. how to get rid of a body
        a. turn it into something else
           i. by declaring that it isn't one
        b. delete it
        c. put it where no one can see it
           i. elsewhere: it isn't a bad place to be

EMPTĪ:
a synonym, apparently. to be from *EMPT*, a land without a
people. a lie.

still governmentally prohibited from going anywhere
i open a webpage   that will show me a livestream
of a window in the world any window any where in the world
i have become accustomed to staying put
          forgotten what being elsewhere does
          to the body
                    heart: beat picks up
fingers and knuckles: they shake

i have tonsillitis

i am on the elsewhere-window webpage
and i have tonsillitis
clicking through like swiping tinder next
next next next   next i am trying
to get myself to palestine
or lebanon or where my parents are
it is snowing in plön germany
it is raining in kochi india
it is also raining in jaipur even though
the two cities are 2.2 thousand kilometers
away from one another
it is not snowing in görwihl germany it is sunny
and the waves look lovely

in melbourne i hear two people having sex out of frame
"this is not elsewhere" next
and now i am in haifa

i rearranged my bedroom in my sharehouse three days ago the
mattress is no longer near the window. all alone i moved my
bed and couch and closet and mirror and clothes rack and now
none of these things are where they were a week ago. i have
slept in my new room twice, both times uncomfortable maybe
because i have tonsillitis and it is affecting the way i breathe
and swallow.

and now i am in haifa
the webpage says haifa israel
and the person's name is annette
so my best guess is that she is a settler
and outside her window looks just like a settlement
so my best guess is that she is a settler

a bird flies across the screen and i say: *huh a metaphor*

i have tonsillitis and it is affecting the way i breathe and
swallow watching a bird fly across the screen in an israeli
settlement and i say: *huh a metaphor*

the sky is blue in haifa today
i sit on the floor of my rearranged bedroom
        the empty space awaiting a new desk
by the window the sky is blue in melbourne
i am thinking: *maybe here and palestine are not so different*
i am thinking: *what is there to miss if both skies are blue?*

before the first pfeilstorch people thought birds in the winter
were gone because they were hibernating

before the first pfeilstorch people thought birds in the winter
were gone because they were under the water and sealed with a
slip of ice

before the first pfeilstorch people thought birds in the winter
were gone because they became a different kind of bird

in 1822 the first pfeilstorch landed near klütz germany with a
thirty-inch spear made of african wood pierced through its
throat. this is when scientists went, a-ha. people realized that
birds in the winter are gone because they are elsewhere.

   15. what marks a people as resilient?
        a. when there are so few of you that the odds can't be good
        b. when there are enough of you to keep each other going

in trying to build a metaphor i end up on the living room floor
scrolling images of dead waterbirds, arrows in their bodies.

in trying to build resilience my parents take me to the movies
when i am still so young, still so shy, in the baby pink hoodie
that zips up and is rhinestoned. together we watch live footage
from the frontlines, a supercut of people dying. boom and then
there is a long ringing. and my little lungs and my little throat
both work in unison to hold on to the breath inside me.

HOW TO MAKE YOUR OWN EXPLOSION

ONE
blow your cheeks out into spheres

TWO
where does the air come from?

THREE
it is not air
it is muscle making room for nothing

twenty-five pfeilstorch have been discovered and taxidermied. they are on display in different parts of the world so close your eyes and think of the great pfeilstorch diaspora. count to twenty-five then open your eyes and keep reading.

EMPTY:
a verb now, as in, emptying something out, genociding.

at work i sign for a parcel. we don't know who sent it. a small
brown cardboard box and inside the box a glass sphere and
inside the glass sphere a fledgling and some formaldehyde. it
sits beside my colleague's computer until we pack up our desks
and go home.

when i check my junk folder there is just a single email in it
subject: annette!
email contents: annette
                https://bit.ly/2Yoj7Zh
                algenoncurrie

i do not trust emails
from strangers
                       especially when there is a link to click

like maybe the settler from the elsewhere-window in haifa has
put me on some kind of list i leave the email in my inbox and
then
DELETE

one more rock thrown
onto the pile to tumble the
mountain on my chest

four hundred and fifty milligrams of nitrate in the groundwater
three hundred   in the wells
nine hundred   in the drinking
                                                                          water

                               all per liter
                               all when the guideline is
fifty   milligrams of nitrate in the groundwater
                                           in the wells
                                         in the drinking
                                                                             water

one thousand
                   eight hundred milligrams of chloride in the wells
six hundred   in the drinking
                                                                     water

                               all per liter
                               all when the guideline is
two hundred and fifty milligrams of chloride in the wells
                                         in the drinking
                                                                     water[12]

watch the settlers
drink the nox-
water and see a body attack
itself acid limb a bitter tongue
                     bitten off and spat out
                           thrashing
on the wet concrete dead
                    fish shallow water

---

12   United Nations Environment Programme, *Environmental Assessment of the Strip*, "Results and Discussions" (Nairobi: United Nations Environment Programme, 2009), 56–62.

too many macaws on a clay lick will make it collapse
clay lick sinks into sea

the entity exports 10.7 million kilograms of dates
palestinian farmhands pick produce
twelve hours a day

10,700,000KG in an israeli pocket

i want to snag a little pit in its gullet
lodged flat and sharp to scratch at tissue

10,700,000KG weighing down the north atlantic on the way
                    to elsewhere a little pit in its windpipe

a holster of lead weighing down the north atlantic on the way
to elsewhere

flying and landing and flying again middle seat red eyes

i am where my parents are but i am on my way out. there are
four flights to tel aviv between 6 and 10PM so i suppose they
must leave every hour. i go through security easily this time but
the man behind me has to have his bag scanned again it's
actually a box it's actually a box packed tight with two 10KG
dumbbells he is on his way to tel aviv twenty kilograms across
the levant twenty kilograms to weigh the airbus down.

i am packing for a move and very sad about it very tired and so
i enter the left half of my hard-shell suitcase the side with
nothing in it yet. i'm prostrate with my eyes closed. i want to
see what it would be like to close it onto my self but the zips
only work from the outside.

16. what's a box?
    a. something you have no power over once you are in it
        i. the atlantic
        ii. a locked closet
        iii. a campfire conversation
        iv. the passenger's seat

i once filled an envelope with shore line rocks and tried to mail them to a friend across the ocean but the post man would not take it the envelope had too many rocks to be a letter.

i went to collect a draft of this book that you are reading but the post man said it didn't exist.

HOW TO MAKE ANOTHER ROCK
please find a piece of paper

ONE
write a letter to settler annette

TWO
delete all words from the letter

THREE
test it out by saying
and

FOUR
scrunch it up

HOW TO MAKE A BOX BACK

ONE
suffocate settler annette

TWO
suffocate the suffocating state

i go to palestine with half my suitcase empty
        and return with it full
        and return with a cardboard box
                labeled FRAGILE
                tightly packed to protect
                the things inside

forty-six kilograms to bring home home

i go to palestine with a new journal
   thought i'd write some metaphors
      but return with scant pages of
                      questions and fodder

the more time i spend with words
the more i realize that they just won't do

   17. what is dawn good for?
     a. a beautiful cusp:
        i. a veil for construction
        ii. a lift for surprise
    gather at dawn
    five hundred gather at dawn
    picket the port of oakland
    block a ship and its boxes
    it's morning then it's afternoon
    then it's six pm and still
    the ship floats bloated
    in the belly of the bay
    keep it heavy
        massive

leave it no choice but to spit up
          and spit out
in glorious explosion
in plains of nonexistence[13]

now i am on the M1 again
with jeanine again
and dangling
from her rearview mirror: a foam cube
          on red string
          a flag on each face
          it is from palestine
she is driving me home

my new apartment has windows that don't open because i
accidentally threw the key out on my second day here windows
that start on one end of the wall and end on the other windows
on both sides of the house windows where the sun can rise into
the kitchen and set in the living room windows that don't open.

i text jeanine, you're back in القُدس right? and she says back in
bethlehem now about to sleep. she's with her fiancé he is trying
to get his west bank ID she is hoping to get one through him
too. unless i marry a palestinian the only means for being pales-
tinian on paper is our liberation. my parents are in the country
i was born in my brother is in his apartment right now working
to make it feel more like home. he bought a rug two weeks ago. i
am in the house with the ghosts again trying to finish this book
wanting to be done with it wanting to move onto the next thing
move on move on.

---

13   Victoria Colliver, David R. Baker, blockade," *SFGate* (June 21, 2010). Accessed
       November 2022: https://www.sfgate.com/bayarea/article/hundreds-in-oak-
       land-protest-gaza-blockade-3260772.php.

sometimes i want to wake up and drive from beirut to haifa
                                or maybe we'll have a ferry

smoke in the golan heights
smoke in lebanon
smoke in the sinai

it's not enough
we're all choking
because empires threatened in 1799 joined
          empires and created their mannequin
              state to break the body limbs
                                splintered black
                                dirt and wet
                                cement blocked
              up weighed down

lebanon to syria
          syria to jordan
              jordan to palestine
                  palestine to egypt
                                splintered black
                                dirt and wet
                                cement blocked
              up weighed down

i am where my parents are
tiles made orange
by tired sun
the air is tired too
unmoving now and my feet are up

three humid swallows
plunging grazing cerulean rising
and then doing it all again

this water is not pure but it is clean, from the chlorine, dad
assures me, it's clean,
three humid swallows
sharpening their wings with bleach

afterword

in 2023 i received a grant from a large state body to travel to the levant and write. i would go to lebanon, cyprus, and palestine, in that order, and while there, work on the edits for this book. i would be gone for three months, returning in late october with the final draft. with what i can only name as intuition, i decided not to go to palestine in the end. instead, i stayed in cyprus two weeks longer and flew back to melbourne two weeks earlier, on october 4, 2023.

as i prepare to send this book to print, i feel anxious about all that has passed since it was completed. the nature of print, palestine, and linear time is that books are read in contexts different from which they were written in. but the acts of violence and resistance in this book align with the acts of violence and resistance taking place as i write this afterword, and the ones taking place as you read it—whenever it is that you're reading it. in november 2023 and well into 2024, protesters blockaded the port of melbourne to stop an israeli freight ship from docking. with this action, i'm reminded of the one written into the end of the book, this time in oakland, and back in 2010. the palestinian struggle long outlives today's and tomorrow's headlines. look, too, to yesterday.

during 2021's unity intifada i drove to the zionist federation in naarm/melbourne with my sister and together we raised cardboard signs. mine read, *you choke palestine*, we choke back. we were heckled by a couple of locals but mostly came away from the action unscathed. it's difficult to articulate what we can do from the global north but essentially, it's to choke back: boycott, stop traffic, turn a ship around, flood the train station. cut off the air supply of imperialism. this is why i fixate on suffocation. this is why i turned it into a book.

this book includes examples of boycott actions and outlines some of our targets. boycotts, divestments, and sanctions (BDS) is a powerful tool that we have been using for decades to isolate the zionist entity of israel and demand its compliance with international law as a bare minimum. in fewer words: it is retaliation.

BDS is beneficial to our fight for liberation because it:

1. is anti-imperial
   a. because it targets multi-million dollar and multi-national companies
      i. many of which are involved in arms trade
2. enables joint-struggle resistance
   a. because these targeted companies are complicit elsewhere, too
      i. other colonies
      ii. other margins
         ١. like ability
         ٢. like gender
         ٣. like class

an earlier draft of the book included a different afterword from this one. much of it was reworded to be integrated into the book itself but i found, even though the text hadn't been deleted, the book still felt like something had been severed. my editor at giramondo described the earlier afterword as a manifesto. i think he was right, and i think it makes sense for the book to have one.

i should also note that BDS neglects to call for the unification of palestinian lands but i can't see our liberation without it. my grandfather was from hittīn but grew up in jish. his father spent ten years working outside of palestine but ultimately returned easily enough. my grandmother made a home in aleppo in her senior years. she used it like refrain, a proxy homeland to come back to before the 2011 syrian war. for many of us, the borders don't mean all that much. when israel attacked lebanon in 2006, we filled every seat of a minivan and rode it to that place in aleppo. my mum's and dad's sides of the family together in the one house—it was not weird. before leaving beirut, my cousin had found our granddad's old sunglasses. bug-eyed, he wore them on the drive, the landscape tinted sepia. once palestine is free, we will fold our flags and place them back in the cupboard. like old scars the borders will flatten. a ferry docks in beirut. a shuttle will park in amman. there's a minivan company and all the drivers are friendly. my brother-in-law fantasizes one hundred years past our liberation, he sees a bullet train.

acknowledgments

I started writing this book on Wurundjeri Country in 2020. But it could be argued that I started writing it when I saw the cattle egret in the dumpster a year prior. Or maybe earlier still, when I stood breathless watching the Great March of Return from my phone. As is the case in this book, time is nonlinear and place is transcendental. Thank you to all the sites that have held me and my family—I find myself in all these places at once. To the Galilee, to Beirut. To Bahrain, the UAE, Cyprus. To Wurundjeri Woi Wurrung Country, Dharug and Gundungurra Country. To the sky. To my body, to my blue suitcase, now broken and replaced.

To Seneca, you saw this as a book before even I did. Thank you for your vision and your hope. Thank you Alison and Evelyn for your poetics and powerful feedback, your guidance was a pillar without which the book would not stand. Thank you Adalya for turning my many anxious drafts into sturdy words that feel more confident and more like me. Thank you Leah for your soft and tough love, and of course your knowledge. Thank you Ivor and the team at Giramondo for your trust in me. Thank you to Jess and Rory from Prototype. Thank you Jeffrey from New Directions for taking the chance with me and this book. Thank you Jenny, Joe, and Joan who each produced beautiful covers for the three editions of this book. Thank you Danny, Carly, Sara, Nasser, and Selina. Thank you Ren for your elation, faith, and flowers, for your wings when they are speckled.

To my siblings, whose perspectives are like gold. Jeanine, thank you for reading draft after draft. Ali, thank you for listening. To my parents, Mohanned and Rida, thank you for the bookshelves you built, boxed and rebuilt time and again.

This book was written with the support of Writers Victoria's Neilma Sidney Literary Travel Fund, Varuna: The National Writers' House, and The Wheeler Centre's Next Chapter Scheme. Thank you to my Next Chapter cohort, to Charlie and Tim in particular, for your camaraderie and encouragement.

Excerpts from this book have been published in *Cordite Poetry Review*, *Australian Poetry Journal*, and the anthology *Heaven Looks Like Us* (Haymarket Books, 2025). Person Books also built a chapbook around the short excerpt performed at *The State of the (Writing) Nation* in 2023. Thank you to the editors of these journals and publishers for your platforms, kindness, and solidarity.

Thank you to Etel Adnan, whose mountains ground me.

HASIB HOURANI, born in Bahrain in 1996, is a Lebanese-Palestinian writer, editor, arts worker, and educator living on Wangal Country in Sydney. His work has appeared in *Meanjin*, *Overland*, *Australian Poetry*, and *Cordite*. Hourani is a 2020 recipient of The Wheeler Centre's Next Chapter Scheme, and his 2021 essay "when we blink" was shortlisted for the Liminal & Pantera Press Nonfiction Prize and published in their 2022 anthology *Against Disappearance*.